OUT *of* BROKENNESS

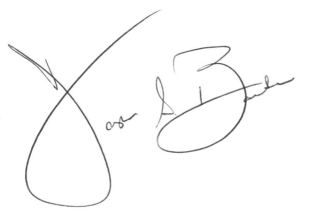

TASHA BASTON

Published, printed, and distributed in the United States by Tasha S. Baston, Valley Stream, New York

Unless otherwise stated, scriptures can be found in the New King James Version of Bible at www.biblegateway.com

Cover Design – Okomota
Editing and Layout – The Self Publishing Maven
Interior Design – Istvan Szabo, Ifj., Sapphire Guardian International
Cover Photo – Alisa Haughton Photography

ISBN 13: 978-1-7336191-0-3

www.tashabaston.org

ACKNOWLEDGMENTS

Several people gave their undying love and support in my moment of brokenness. I am grateful for every prayer, every caregiver, every cook, every transporter, every groomer, and the list goes on. Thank you from the bottom of my heart. I know I couldn't have made it through many moments without angels like you.

Adrell McDonald
Alcita and Issac Zellner
Andrew Smiley
Apostle Elise Banks
Ashari James
Aunt Elaine and Uncle Schaffer
Aunt Ivy Floyd
Bishop Darren and Kim Ferguson
Bishop Martin and Gail Watson
Camille Hibbert
Charles Staunton
Dr. Doris Shackelford
Electra Nicholson
Elder Sharod Tomlinson
Jamel Robinson
Jan Fennell
Jason Tomlinson
Joann Manley
Kellie Quarles

Khristine Gordon
Kimberly Martin
Linda Phinazee
Michael and Laverne Baston
Monique Sidberry
Nina Ware
Peggy Picou
Petia Guthrie
Rob Siracusano
Sheree Page
Taysa Clarke
Tynisa Martin

Thank you to my literary pusher, my Robin Devonish, for the gentle nudges when I did not feel like completing this assignment.

DEDICATION

I dedicate this book to:

My warrior, my King, my confidant, my covering, my husband, my best friend, and My Do Me Right Bishop Dr. Michael A. Baston. I LOVE YOU!

My strong, my courageous, my favorite girl and mother, Hertel Boyd. Thank you for all your love, care and for believing in me.

To those who have broken moments and places in their life, I pray my story gives you a testament to the Lord's healing power in all our lives.

Please enjoy the journey of being YOU.

FOREWORD

Maya Angelou once said, "Having courage does not mean that we are unafraid. Having courage and showing courage means we face our fears. We are able to say, I have fallen, but I will get up." I believe that my wife, Tasha Sharron Baston is one of the most courageous women I've ever met in my life. I literally watched her pick up the broken pieces of her physical body, while holding together the fractured elements of her self-confidence due to a horrific and avoidable accident. She could have retreated into herself. She could have been swallowed up by and deposited in the cage of her emotions. She could have given up, given out, and given in. Instead, she held onto the belief that God had more for her to accomplish in life. She trusted that there would be a way back to normalcy. She looked fear and doubt in the eyes and introduced them to her fact -- she is more than a conqueror.

I was attracted to Tasha's beautiful smile, warmth, sassiness, love for God, and her golden voice. In introducing her to others, I would often say that when she opened her mouth, the angels in heaven would hoist up the window and hang over the ledge to hear her sing. More than her singing, I came to learn quite quickly that there was a prophetic insight in Tasha. She could read people like a book. And more importantly, the desire of her heart was that people would be saved, set free, and delivered. I knew early on she was the woman I wanted to spend the rest of my life with.

We lived a good life. We had great plans. We saw ourselves moving forward. When her mother became ill, Tasha doing the noble thing, suspended her studies for her master's degree. A few years later when Tasha's mother recovered, she went back to finish her degree. One thing about my wife, she's a person that always seeks to finish the things she starts. I would never have imagined that fighting so hard to get back in school would ultimately result in the tragic injury by way of a gas explosion at the college.

I received a frantic call that my wife was wounded from a building implosion. My heart pounded. Many thoughts raced through my mind. But one thing I knew was that God would not take her from me. I knew that she had not left to go to heaven because I would have felt it in the city of my soul. I raced through Queens and somehow flew over the George Washington Bridge to get to the local hospital. There I learned that my Tasha had completely shattered her leg. Thankfully all her other vital signs and organs we're in good condition. But that hospital simply did not have the skill to begin the process of helping her to get reconstruction. We moved her to the neighboring county hospital's critical care unit. Over many hours of surgery, and multiple days in that hospital, I watched the beginning of the very arduous journey that my wife would take to get back to herself.

For anyone who has ever had a tragic life circumstance happen to them. Anyone whose plans were interrupted. For anyone who found themselves in the position of needing to become a comeback kid. To anyone who's ever found the need to be the hero of their own story, my wife's testimony in *Out of Brokenness* will give you some insight on how to have the courage you need to overcome anything. I hope you enjoy this letter of faith, hope, and love.

Bishop Dr. Michael A. Baston,
Husband and President, Tasha S. Baston Fan Club
Presiding Prelate, Called to the Nations Covenant Churches Intl.,
Senior Pastor, St. Luke Cathedral,
President, Rockland Community College

PREFACE

The word 'broken' has different meanings for different people. However, what about when something comes in your life where you are literally 'broken?' I mean hurt, shattered to where massive healing and mending must take place. I don't want to get too far ahead, so please allow me to tell you a little about myself.

I am Prophetess Tasha Sharron Baston, from Orlando, Florida, wife to Bishop, Dr. Michael A. Baston, CEO, mentor, activist, and Leading Lady of St. Luke's Cathedral in Laurelton, New York. I am also the founder of Tasha Baston Ministries, The Breaker Anointing Experience, and W.I.N.G.S. (Women Impacting the Next Generation of Sisters).

My mother raised me to be independent, and one who lives a life pleasing to God. From a young child, God has had me on this journey of seeing dreams and visions concerning people, places and things. As I have grown into a woman, learning of God and His calling, I have embraced the prophetic gift He has given me.

I believe it's important to share that part of me because once you read my story, you may think, well, if she is prophetic, why didn't she see that coming? My answer is as simple as the scripture which says, "For we know in part, and we prophesy in part." –1 Corinthians 13:9

God may not reveal everything to you, but if you are in a relationship with Him, He can show you how to get through any moment of surprise, trauma, and battle.

I decided to share my story because many people have or will experience trauma or circumstances that has or will alter their lives forever. I understand the literal physical and emotional pain one endures and how uncomfortable, confined, lonely, frustrating, depressing, and fearful one may feel while flowing on a roller coaster ride of uncertainty about the future. However, I also know that in all things good and bad, there is a process we must go through to get through, and the scriptures are true (read at your leisure) in Isaiah 54:11, Isaiah 58:8, and Philippians 4:13.

Adversity is tied to purpose. Adverse times provide the opportunity to find yourself amid the pain. It's also the best time to focus on God, handle your emotions, seek to heal and discover your destiny. You may not believe it, but destiny becomes clearer in adversity. I wrote this book with a few goals in mind:

1. Share my journey through a traumatic and life-altering experience.
2. Share how I found myself during pain.
3. Teach how to go to a place of peace and release within a situation.
4. Show how we are never alone. God is with us even when we can't seem to find Him.
5. To pray if you are in a season of despair.

I must share this disclaimer and say this book is not in order of events, but the day to day order of my temporarily broken mind, vision, spirit, and how the hand of God was with me. I invite you to turn the page and read my story of how I stepped "Out of Brokenness."

"It is when believers are out of answers, confidence and strength, with nowhere else to turn but to God that they are in a position to be most effective. No one in the kingdom of God is too weak to experience God's power, but many are too confident in their own strength. Physical suffering, mental anguish, disappointment, unfulfillment, and failure squeeze the impurities out of believers' lives making them pure channels in which God's power can flow."

– John MacArthur

CONTENTS

FIRM FOUNDATION

I understand that everyone didn't have Jesus in their life, all their life. However, for me, I have.

I remember my first encounter with God as early as the age of three. I went to church with my mother and recall singing on the children's choir. I sang so hard that my voice rang louder than the other children. I was eventually put off the choir for my loudness (chuckle).

At age seven, my parents were in the process of divorcing. My mother had to work on Sunday and didn't have anyone she could trust to take me to church. I would often cry because I wanted to go, not to hang with the other kids; I was drawn to God's presence.

At age eight, I went to the altar with my mom and confessed Christ as Savior. I gave the pastor my right hand to signify fellowship, was baptized and placed on the young adult choir since I had such a big voice. Sunday school, vacation Bible school, Christian summer camp, if it was about Jesus, I was there.

At age fourteen, one Sunday I visited a church with a group of friends who had a great youth ministry. I went again and encouraged my mother to come with me. After the service ended, I shared I wanted to switch churches. After some prayer, she agreed, and we switched to St. Mark A.M.E Church with a Pentecostal feel. I was blossoming, singing in the choir, and then suddenly I had an inexpressible encounter with God while leading a song.

By the age of eighteen, while attending Edward Waters College, prayer became my burden. I wanted God all the time and couldn't wait to read my Bible and get into His presence. At this point, I went to church with my godparents because my school wasn't near my home church. I wasn't active there because I began feeling like I wanted to be a regular teenager, which wasn't good. Distractions and rebellion took over for a moment, and I backslid.

I know you thought there wouldn't be a detour in the story, but remember, we all have come short of God's glory. I found my way back, switched schools, and met a friend from Queens, New York who told me about Apostle John Boyd. I had never heard of him and had no idea he would take part in my spiritual growth years later.

The Lord began to deal with me, and I would go through bouts of uncontrollable crying and Him ministering to me in my dreams. One recurring dream I recall is of me riding my bike into a field of flowers with a dog running beside me. In 1997, I told my mother that I wanted to move to New York. Upon my arrival, I stayed with my aunt. One day I went to visit my grandmother in the nursing home, and while there, I saw a picture of a little girl with the same elements of my dream. Thank God for confirmation!

My new home church was First Corinthian Baptist Church. Later I created a gospel singing group named Infinite Praise and attended 5:00 a.m. prayer gatherings regularly with a few of my friends. The awesome spiritual encounters with God continued, and at times I would rent a hotel room so that I could have quiet communication with the Lord.

In 2002, I became a member of Bronx Community Baptist Church and was licensed as a minister. I also enrolled at Berkeley College to continue my education and met my now-husband Dr. Michael A. Baston. In 2006, he became the Pastor of St. Luke Cathedral in Queens, New York. I finally met Apostle Boyd in 2007, and we became closer in 2010. In 2012, he consecrated my husband as Bishop and me Prophetess. Apostle passed a few months later. In 2012, I was installed as the Co-Pastor of our church.

> **"Therefore whoever hears these sayings of Mine, and does them, I will liken him to a wise man who built his house on the rock, and the rain descended, the floods came, and the winds blew and the beat on that house; and it did not fall, for it was founded on the rock."**
>
> **– Matthew 7:24-25**

I share this scripture here because I believe I have stood on a firm foundation with Christ, which equips one to endure the good, bad, the indifferent and when things are silent. I've been blessed to have spiritual teachers, mentors, fathers, and mothers who helped guide me in the Lord. I am grateful for First Lady Sheila Jenkins, Mildred Dixon, Apostle Elise Banks, and my natural mother Hertel, who is awesome; she has always supported me in going forth with God. However, my firm foundation was literally shaken where many questions were asked, and the answers came slowly.

BROKEN MIND

HOW DID I GET HERE?

Tuesday, June 4, 2013 is a day forever grained in my mind. I was attending college pursuing my degree and was inside my dean's office on the 2nd floor talking about my thesis. Suddenly, there was an explosion in the building which caused it to shake, and smoke appeared.

As I tried to make a way of escape, the staircase imploded. Debris was everywhere as the building's beams began to fall. The was no more staircase. The air became thick. Outside onlookers were calling forth, urging our survival. I thought, 'would the building completely collapse? How much time did we have left? What about my husband? My mother?

This can't be how my story would end.' I had to take a leap of faith for my family. I had to take a leap of faith for my future. I had to take a leap of faith for my life. Once out of the horror of the doomed building through a window, I landed on the concrete flat-footed severely shattering my leg and changing my world. I was rushed to the hospital and had to have emergency surgery. The result rendered me incapacitated and unable to walk. In a matter of 12 hours, my entire life shifted, and my mind was blown.

How did I get to this place of the unknown?
How did I get to this place of trauma?
How did I get to this place of pain?

We often hear there are stages to grief; however there are also stages to dealing with trauma. Before I go any further, I think it's important to define the word 'Trauma.' It means, "A deeply distressing or disturbing experience; emotional shock following a stressful event or a physical injury, which may be associated with physical shock and sometimes leads to long-term neurosis." Yes, I believe God and His healing power. However, I had to know in what areas I needed to be healed. A physical part of my body was shattered; however, emotional and psychological trauma were there as well. I submit that it's important to know what you are going through not just spiritually, but naturally.

The stages of trauma are (1) Safety and Stabilization (2) Remembrance and Mourning (3) Reconnection and Integration. For further elaboration, I encourage you to visit http://trauma-recovery.ca/recovery/phases-of-trauma-recovery/. While these phases apply to me, I must describe my self-defined phases of trauma which were:

- ❖ Shock
- ❖ Impatience/Understanding
- ❖ Isolation
- ❖ Moving Forward

Shock – I couldn't believe what was happening. My good life, career, and ministry were flourishing. I was walking blessed with good health, a great marriage, a thriving ministry, and in pursuit of my college degree. Why me? How did I go from thriving to total dependency and incapacitation? I was quickly propelled into a place of humiliation and humility. I was quickly forced to roll with the punches and adapt to the shock.

8

Impatience/Understanding – I understood what I was going through but wanted it all to be over. Especially when I was told my process of healing would be a very long one, a deep restlessness set in. I also believed that no one understood how I felt, which led to an inner impatience that couldn't be expressed.

Isolation – God longed for me, and I had to answer the call to His presence. I spent a lot of alone time and learning how to get from 'here' to 'there.'

Moving Forward – Surgeries, Physical Therapy, and Therapy (Yes, Counseling) and Healing were necessary for me to move from tragedy to triumph.

Getting There

When the accident occurred, I developed coping mechanisms to get through the beginning moments. I protected my mind from overload, thought constructively, and consistently declared I would live and not die. The poking, prodding, doctors, nurses, diagnoses, timelines, and various moments can get to you. However, after a point I had to understand the reality of what was happening and how my life was forever changed.

What is There? Getting 'there' is a place of acceptance without feeling defeated. My reality of 'there' was, I couldn't walk and wouldn't for a while. I had to be waited on hand and foot. The sooner I was able to understand those two factors; I could move forward to getting 'there' where total healing from brokenness could take place.

Despite the questions, shock, restlessness, disbelief, confusion, and anger, I knew deep down that God had His hand on me. I had to go through this season (Ecclesiastes 3) of getting to know Tasha. A self-assessment was necessary, and I had to see some things.

First, it could've been worse! Picture this! I jumped out of a 2nd floor window and landed on my feet. The only thing that happened was a Pilon Fracture of my Right Leg, and my Right Ankle Fibula and Tibia were broken. I could've landed on my head, broke my neck or even died, but I shattered my leg. Yes, it's an inconvenient and painful big deal, but I had a moment of understanding. Also, there was nothing I could do about what happened. The only thing I could do was move toward healing.

Second, having anger is fine! It was okay to be real about my anger, my feelings and unafraid to share with others. Within the body of Christ and the black community we believe that only a certain type of person needs therapy or counseling. To be further transparent, my thoughts were, 'how can you sit with a counselor when people come to you (though confined to a bed) for counsel?' Incapacitation and confinement can play on one's psyche. To process all that I was dealing with, I needed the Lord and a Therapist! Time out for self-righteousness! Time out for judging the very people that could help me heal!

Third 'Spiritual Endurance' was necessary! After being released from the hospital, I had a long road ahead of me, and the Lord was silent on of how I got there.

There is a myth in Christian faith that because we confess Christ, nothing in our lives should happen. Although on a journey to getting 'there,' I had bouts of depression, despair, distress, and wondered how I was going to survive. I needed clarity.

Prayer for Clarity – 2 Kings 6:17 "And Elisha prayed, and said, Lord, I pray open his eyes, that he may see." And the Lord opened the eyes of the young man; and he saw: and, behold, the mountain was full of horses and chariots of fire all around Elisha."

Father, in Jesus name, open my eyes that I may have clarity in this present moment. Help me to know that the clarity I'm receiving from you is not to shake my faith, but to increase my faith and fully put my trust in you. Father, thank you for guiding me and opening my spirit to know that you are always by my side! Amen.

PARANOIA

Trauma can bring paranoia. "Nightmares, unwanted memories of the trauma, avoiding situations that bring back memories, anxiety, and a depressed mood," are all of what I experienced. Not to mention, taking pain killers reinforced the fear because some medications had the side effect of hallucinations. The enemy was on his job to exacerbate my thoughts and feelings to the point where I felt like, at times, I was losing it.

I believe that the paranoia came to break my faith in God.

When having another surgery, the doctors would say, "There is a chance you won't wake up from the anesthesia." I was told regularly that I wouldn't be normal or walk without assistance again. I was given several declarations; however, I 'CANCELLED' all those words, feelings, and understood exactly what was going on. I said, "Tasha, you're not going to die because you have yet to fulfill anything!"

I daily decreed and declared the promises of God over my life with boldness. I listened to music that calmed my thoughts and spirit. I created moments of thanks and worship to the Lord. My level of discernment heightened, and I became keenly aware of what was going on around me so I could nip it in the bud. Whatever I didn't have inside me to fight, I asked the Lord to impart and ignite His spirit in me further. Also, I solicited prayers from both my biological and spiritual mothers.

During my bouts with paranoia, I had two revelations from God.

The first one was 'God will take us to boot camp without preparation.' Who learns how to go through tests and trials beforehand? We can learn a few things by seeing others go through, but the raw teaching comes in how you handle the trial. The second one was 'midnight only lasts for a minute.' There's 12:00 a.m., then there's 12:01, meaning it's no longer midnight. My revelation for this, 'Tasha, all of this is temporary.'

Whatever you are going through right now say, 'All of this is temporary!' I know it's hard, but don't focus on your situation; focus on God, who is the mind regulator.

Prayer for A Sound Mind – 2 Timothy 1:7 "For God has not given us a spirit of fear; but of power, and of love and of a sound mind."

God, I thank you for keeping my mind on You! When I keep my heart and mind on you, then you will give me perfect peace, which will lead my mind to soundness. I thank you for removing the fear and doubt from my mind and releasing your power, love, and authority over me right now, in the name of Jesus! Amen.

BROKEN VISION

WHEN WILL THE SUN RISE AGAIN?

Was the lingering question I had for God but never received a response. The scripture Jeremiah 29:11 is clear in telling us God knows the plans He has for us. However, it's a challenge to see the sun (or son) when your life takes a drastic and sudden shift. I had to rest in depending on friends and family for the simple things, which didn't feel good.

I was in the hospital for 23 days before being released to go home. While there, I had two surgeries. The first one was an emergency when rushed to the hospital on the day of the implosion. The operation consisted of inserting a Fixater to keep my leg in place. Once finished, I developed an infection and the pain was excruciatingly indescribable. I was given medication for the infection which delayed my second surgery. Once I received the okay, and the infection was gone, the second operation was to put in a plate, screws, and pins to further hold my leg together. In those 23 days, I couldn't shower, walk to the bathroom located inside my room, or hygienically care for myself without assistance. I went from independent to dependent and from caretaker to being cared for on the daily things we take for granted. The Lord wasn't talking when I asked why or how long.

To prepare for my release, the nurses taught me how to give myself injections to prevent blood clots in my body. I endured 60 days of needles in my stomach.

Has that ever happened where you waited on God for answers, and He didn't say a word? Though I felt like the sun (son) was setting on me at times, God continuously gave me rays of light. Psalm 84:11 "For the Lord God is a sun and shield; The Lord will give grace and glory; No good thing will He withhold from those who walk uprightly."

Rays of Light

Sunrise is the most beautiful time of the day. It declares that new is coming and anything wonderful can happen that day. The best way to describe how I held on is by the rays of light I received from God and others.

Although I felt darkness often, people would tell me I look beautiful or how I didn't look like what I'd been through on a day where I felt my worst. My husband, mother, family, and friends brought their rays of light as well. I believe that God shows His presence the most when He sends people, you would normally see in passing, to your doorstep to love on and encourage you.

One day while home, my doorbell rang, and I couldn't believe who I saw when she walked in. I don't want to say her name because of discretion, but this evangelist and woman of God, who I highly respect and look up to, came to sit with and encourage me. I didn't expect that because I normally see her in passing at church services. I am grateful to her and God for that special visit.

Tragedy tends to bring a heightened sense of awareness of God's greatness. We pay more attention to everything that is going on around us. For me, it was those rays of light where I believe God was displaying and saying, "Trust me Tasha. I know what you need, and I got you!"

Prayer for Trusting God When He Doesn't Answer – Psalm 62:1-2 "Truly my soul silently waits for God; From Him comes my salvation. He only is my rock and salvation; He is my defense; I shall not be greatly moved."

Father, I thank you for building my trust in you, while I wait patiently for my prayer request to be answered. Thank you for helping me to know that you have everything under control. God, help me to hold on to my faith in you as you work everything out on my behalf (even if you don't answer when I feel you should). Please keep me grounded in your will and word. Thank you for reminding me that your answer is working for my purpose, in Jesus name! Amen.

ROLLER COASTER
LIKE NO OTHER

As a young person, I loved riding the roller coaster. My favorite two were Big Thunder and Space Mountain. When at the amusement park, they were my first choices, and I was comfortable with them because I knew when each dip, twist, curve, and turn was coming. The Space Mountain ride was dark, but stars in the fake sky illuminated the ride. Like most coasters, going up was slow, but going down is fast, low, and then the ride levels. Emotions are all over the place, but the thrill and exhilaration are everything. We believe the ride will be safe with no mechanical issues.

Going through my process of mending, I felt like I was on a roller coaster. However, I didn't like the ride at all. I had new rules and triggers like leaving any building I believed smelled like gas. My emotions were uncontrollable at times and leveling out wasn't in sight.

It's interesting how life changes and the things you once took for granted, you learn to appreciate the blessing of once havin it. My highs on the ride were, doing some things on my own like going to the restroom without assistance, being home by myself, going out to the mall or a restaurant, and being able to preach again. My lows on the ride were surgeries, intense pain, and health issues unrelated to my leg. Did my situation begin to level out? Yes, once I began to trust God throughout the process.

Life is a ride of ups, downs, twists, turns, curves and some darkness! What have I learned about being on this roller coaster? Embrace the ride! Acceptance is a powerful tool when used correctly and not in defeat. The key is to ask, 'now that I've accepted the situation, what can I do to heal, adapt or become a different person while on the ride?' Testify! Most times when you get off a roller coaster, the people waiting in line will ask, how was the ride? And, we gladly answer the question. Our ride is designed to tell others about the great and powerful Jesus. At the time of riding, one may not see it that way, but I'm sure you've heard our tests are not for us, but others. Know that you are secure in Jesus! When you ride on the coaster, the seats are secure so that you won't fall out. There are seat belts and bars that work to ensure your safety. The secure seat is our directive that we must abide in the covering of God. Just like we believe the ride won't fail, we must maintain our faith and believe in our God, who never fails.

Prayer for Adapting to Change and Sudden Transition – Philippians 4:11-12 "Not that I speak in regard to need, for I have learned in whatever state I am, to be content: I know how to be abased, and I know how to abound. Everywhere and in all things, I have learned both to be full and to be hungry, both to abound and to suffer need."

Father in Jesus' name, I thank you that in times of the unfamiliar and in times of change, you are teaching me to be content and to trust your process. Lord, thank you for teaching me that I can make it through any circumstance, situation, and changes that I may face. Even when sudden transitions take place in my life Father, thank you for going before me, being with me, not failing me, or forsaking me. Thank you for reminding me not to fear and that everything is in your hand and your care! Lord, please continue to keep me knowing how to be abased and abound In Jesus name! Amen.

EARTH ANGELS

In your darkest times, the Lord will place people in your life who will step up and cover you. They will sacrifice their money, time, attention, and whatever is needed to make sure you're okay.

An 'Earth Angel' is someone who often unexpectedly becomes a source of inspiration and support at a time when you need it most.

Once it was understood the amount of help necessary to have an ounce of normalcy, God dispatched His 'Earth Angels' to care for my husband and me.

Without asking, many came to cook, clean, and care for me and our home. Others took turns taking me to doctors, therapy, and physical therapy appointments. Two of our godsons decided to move in with us to help.

Being a proud and independent, but not a puffed-up person, the amount of help received was overwhelming and a lot to breathe in. I saw, in real-time, how much I am loved.

Due to their sacrifice, I received two revelations. First, God will send help, but we allow our pride to block the blessing. Second, how important it is to embrace the provision made for you in whatever season you are in.

The word of God rings true, which says, "Greater love has no one than this than to lay down one's life for his friends." – John 15:13

LET US PRAY

Coming out of brokenness requires much faith, studying the Word of God, and a prayer life. During my process of emotional and physical healing, I had to draw on the scriptures and exercise my ability to pray often and sometimes quickly depending on what was happening from moment to moment. Prayer provides direction, eradicates anxiety, thwarts distractions, sharpens our discernment, and yields peace. Let us continue to pray with each other.

Help To Fervently Pray

James 5:16 "Confess your trespasses to one another, and pray for one another, that you may be healed. The effective, fervent prayer of the righteous man avails much."

Father, I thank you for igniting in me a deep, focused, enthusiastic prayer life that will allow me to commune and be in alignment with you and your word! Thank you Lord, for the new intensity that is upon my life now, In Jesus name! Amen.

Prayer To Connect With God

John 15:5-7 "I am the vine, you are the branches. He who abides in Me and I in him, bears much fruit; for without Me you can do nothing. If anyone does not abide in Me, he is cast out as a branch and is withered; and they gather them and throw them into the fire, and they are burned. If you abide in Me, and My words abide in you, you will ask what you desire, and it shall be done for you."

Father, I thank you for my connection with you. Thank you for the reminder: if I remain in you and you in me that I will produce the will you have for my life. God, as I join into my intimate time in your word and your presence, I appreciate knowing that you will always be consistent in me. I thank you for when I remain in you, you hear my heartbeat, and you answer. In Jesus name! Amen.

Praying To Focus On God

Colossians 3:2 "Set your mind on things above, not on things on the earth."

Lord, I come to you, thanking you, for allowing me to come to a place where I'm able to focus on you. Lord, help me not to be distracted when I submit myself in prayer, fasting, and consecration with you! I declare that my time with you will be sacred and I will bring myself under subjection to receive your overwhelming presence. For I know, when I focus on you, my heart and spirit will be at peace! I decree this to be so in Jesus' name! Amen.

Prayer for Destiny

Jeremiah 29:11 "For I know the thoughts that I think toward you says the Lord, thoughts of peace and not of evil, to give you a future and a hope."

Father, we thank you for having our life and destiny in your hands! We know that your thoughts aren't our thoughts, and your ways aren't our ways, but you all ways supersede the requests that lie upon our hearts and desires. So today, we thank you for filling us with peace, joy, and unimaginable favor for our destiny, In Jesus' name! Amen.

Prayer For The Promise

Hebrews 10:23 "Let us hold fast the confession of our hope without wavering, for He who promised is faithful."

Lord, I thank you for being faithful concerning your promises. I ask in the name of Jesus that you strengthen me as I hold fast to my profession of working my faith without doubt or worry. I thank you that you are a promise keeper, and whatever you speak, it is established! In Jesus Name! Amen.

Prayer Against Fear

Deuteronomy 31:8 "And the Lord, He is the One who goes before you. He will be with you. He will not leave you nor forsake you; do not fear or be dismayed."

Father, in Jesus' name, I thank you right now that you are covering me with the Blood of Jesus and uprooting every fear, phobia and traumatic event that has taken place in my life. Father, I thank you and trust that you will open my eyes to be able to discern when danger, or a threat, is near. I believe that you will shield me from every tormenting spirit, that could cause me to go back into a place of hiding and stagnancy. Thank you Lord that I am set free from every trap and every feeling of fear In Jesus' name, Amen!

Prayer for Peace

Philippians 4:7 "And the peace of God, which surpasses all understanding, will guard your hearts and minds through Christ Jesus."

Father, right now I thank you for the release of peace upon my life, in the name of Jesus! Everything that has disturbed my life and has caused me to be worried, overloaded and overwhelmed, I cast it out in the name of Jesus! I ask that you blanket me now with your understanding. I am trusting You in every aspect of my life, in Jesus' Name! Amen.

Prayer Against Feelings of Loneliness

Isaiah 41:10 "Fear not, for I am with you; Be not dismayed for I am your God. I will strengthen you, Yes, I will help you, I will upload you with My righteous hand."

God, I thank you that in times of distress, confusion, darkness, and unpleasant emotions you are always there with me. I thank you, for your very presence reminds me not to fear in any circumstance I may find myself in. I know you will strengthen and uphold me. Father, thank you for the reminder that You have not given me the spirit of fear, but love, power, and a sound mind, for that, I thank you! In Jesus name! Amen.

Prayer Against Feeling Depressed

Psalm 40:1-3 "I waited patiently for the Lord; And He inclined to me And heard my cry. He also brought me up out of a horrible pit, Out of the miry clay, And set my feet upon a rock, And stabled my steps. He has put a new song in my mouth – Praise to our God; Many will see it and fear, And will trust in the Lord."

Heavenly Father, I thank you for delivering me from feeling down and depressed. I thank you for hearing my cry and answering me with the comfort of your voice. When the enemy came to destroy my emotions and attempted to destroy my faith in you, you heard me and came to rescue me from that horrible pit. For that, I am thankful. I am blessed by the new song you have put in my mouth! I will forever praise you for all you have done! Thank You Lord! In Jesus Name! Amen.

Prayer For Covenant Relationships

Genesis 31:44 "Now therefore, come, let us make a covenant you and I, and let it be a witness between you and me."

Father in the name of Jesus, thank you for all the covenant relationships you have allowed me to be a part of and for the ones in the future. God, as you allow these covenants to form please show me how I can be a blessing to every person you allow me to be in covenant with. As you present new covenants, please show me how to build a loyal commitment that will provide openness and truth. Lord, I thank you for your example of unconditional love and kindness. I thank you in advance for helping me to rise into new dimensions of love, deep admiration, and harmony In Jesus name! Amen.

BROKEN SPIRIT

BATTLE TESTED

Warfare is real! Adversities come to test our battle skills. Think about a soldier who enlists to protect their country. Training must take place, and they learn how to fight before going into battle. They learn about the forms of protection like their vests, helmets, and weapons. They're also taught to listen and discern when their enemy is coming toward them. Soldier candidates have a series of tests and milestones they are required to pass before going into full combat.

I believe the above is what God requires of us to be prepared. We must be tested to know what forms of protection to use. In battle, we have fasting, praise, prayer, scripture, singing of hymns, worship, and the blood of Jesus to plead. Incorporating our protections allows us to discern when the enemy is attacking our mind (talking to us), our body (with pain), our spirit (when we feel week, and unable to pray).

The enemy speaks more when it seems like God is quiet. Therefore, I was clear my accident was a direct attempt to break my spirit and thwart the promise of God for my life. My newly appointed position in the Lords' church as Prophetess (in 2012) had to be tested. From that one day, all the past prophecies I received and intimate moments with the Lord were subject for questioning due to the state I was in.

While going through my process, I was further 'Battle Tested' and often. Additional biopsies and tests for Breast

Cancer, surgeries on my breasts to remove cysts, gall bladder surgery, and emergency dental work, during the healing of my leg, further tested my faith. At times I suffered from separation anxiety when thinking about the possibility of leaving my husband or mother here. And when that happened, God was faithful to send many, even one of my doctors, to tell me to keep on believing.

My discernment remained on constant alert. The Bible tells us to watch and pray; therefore, I was equipped with my prayer shawl and did battle, within the third and fourth prayer watches, if necessary. And if there were times I couldn't pray, I tuned into anointed services online, worshipped and read books of those who teach on warfare like, Apostle John Eckhardt, Dr. Cindy Trimm, Frank Milligan, Barbie Breathett and James Goll.

Regardless of what is thrown our way, the fight is fixed because the Lord has His army of angels fighting for us; He and they will never be defeated.

A Warriors Prayer – Ephesians 6:10-11 "Finally, my brethren, be strong in the Lord, and in the power of his might. Put on the whole armor of God that you may be able to stand against the wiles of the devil."

Father in Jesus' name, I thank you for equipping me and endowing my life with the supernatural tools of the full armor of God! I am now covered with The Belt of Truth, The Breastplate of Righteousness, The Gospel of Peace, The Shield of Faith, The Helmet of Salvation and The Sword of the Spirit! I come against every spirit of fear, illusion, torment, emotionalism, pain, frustration, confusion, distractions, and consumption of darkness Now in The Name of Jesus! Amen.

FEELING OUT OF PLACE

My role as the Co-Pastor of St. Luke Cathedral was very involved. I am a person who likes to know everything so that the church can glorify God in how we serve and interact with His people. My husband and I had a great balance of ministry duties due to him working full-time as well. However, six months would pass before I could return to church again, and those times of attendance weren't consistent.

Before the accident, I worked with the staff to put certain systems in place, etc. However, when I returned, I felt dysfunctional, literally with nothing to contribute. I wasn't needed since so much had progressed in my absence. Don't get me wrong, I know the world doesn't revolve around me and life must keep moving, but I want to be transparent in how I felt in my human moment.

After drawing closer to the Lord, He showed me that I needed to be relieved of those responsibilities so I could be clearer for my prophetic gift. My presence was needed elsewhere for praying, preaching, prophesying, and encouraging. He decided to move me from the position of being hands on to a position of overseeing.

During this process of feeling out of place, I decided I didn't want to go back to preaching. I felt inadequate because I couldn't stand and move around the way I was used to.

I shared my thoughts with my husband, therapist, and other advisors. I am grateful they rallied around me and gave encouragement of why I needed to keep fighting and going. God used them to help me see people needed to hear God's word despite the state I was in.

Eventually, I found a new direction of understanding that I'm not a superwoman. Though I had the limitation of standing, God was developing a new way of displaying His power through me. Upon the revelations I received via conversing with others, I asked the Lord to show me all the broken areas that needed to be mended so I wouldn't feel out of place but be where He wanted. The Lord dealt with how I felt, and I surrendered to the process, He poured more into me so I could be a blessing to others and do whatever He willed to glorify His name.

Prayer for the Process – Philippians 1:6 "Being confident of this very thing, that He who has begun a good work in you will complete it until the day of Jesus Christ;"

Father God, in the name of Jesus, I thank you that you have given me confidence throughout this process. I know that you are aware of the beginning and the end. Help me to understand that you are working in me and stretching me into a new mindset and authority in the realm of the spirit. God, as I walk through this process of understanding, let me be reminded that the good work you started in me will be perfected, In Jesus name! Amen.

THAT'LL PREACH!

IT'S IN YOU!

From the womb, God deposits certain 'gifts' that can be used later if we become aware, embrace it, and tap into what He has given us. For me, it was open visions and seeing demonic spirits.

As early as eight years old, I remember a few demonic and open vision encounters which frightened me. The enemy used my fear to distort my abilities, and I suppressed what God was attempting to do in me. However, those 'gifts' never left but rested until I could begin to handle the magnitude of what they carried.

While attending college in Florida, it was no secret to my dorm mates that I prayed often. One day, there was a student who appeared to have a demonic spirit on them. My college mates were fearful and decided to call me to cast it out. Now, who told them I could do what they were asking? Not me! However, the 'gift' in me quickly rose, and I did what was asked without fear.

Fast forward to 2013, after my accident was probably the biggest test to tap into the 'gifts' the Lord gave me. However, the Lord added the title of a 'warrior' to the 'gifts' given.

In my moments of surgeries and immobility, the Lord had to further show me how to be mobile in the spirit and the importance of seeking Him more than ever. He wanted to take me from the broken place of sadness, being hurt and all that went with it. Furthermore, He showed me how to regain my purpose through the process.

Why am I saying? God gave you a few 'gifts,' and it's time to dig up and reveal what's in you! Perhaps you are going through something confusing, painful and you're not sure if you have more energy to fight. However, I declare what God has put inside of you is still in you! It's time to tap in, Tap In, TAP IN!!

Watch this! If you spell 'Tap' backward, it spells 'Pat,' and I see Him patting you on the back saying, 'Come closer and focus on Me. I have all the power to heal your wounds. Walk it out with me! Remember my words in Psalm 23. Trust me there is growth in the valley. I have equipped you to withstand it all. It's In You!'

Prayer for Release – Proverbs 4:25-26 "Let your eyes look straight ahead, and your eyelids look right before you. Ponder the path of your feet And let all your ways be established."

I thank you Father in Jesus' name for a sudden release of supernatural insight into my situation! God, I declare and decree a release from heartache, disappointment, pressure, unsettledness, pain in my body, mental confusion and darkness. I thank you for releasing joy and perseverance upon me, to fulfill every assignment you give me in Jesus name. I command It to be so NOW! Amen.

THE HAND OF GOD

THE BREAKING POINT

Though I prayed and believed God, I came to a time of breaking. I could no longer accept or deal with all that was going on. I fought hard, but the weight was taking over. After a year of going through, I was over it, spent, strained and felt like I was going to snap.

I was sleeping and living between my kitchen and living room in a hospital bed because I couldn't climb the stairs of my house or enjoy the modern convenience of taking a shower whenever I wanted.

I had occasions of uncontrollable weeping and depression. Although not abandoned, I believed I was; and my beliefs married the spirit of rejection. My husband didn't know what or who he was coming home to when returning from work each day. Sidebar, Michael, I appreciate and love you for loving me through that space.

I became frustrated with my disabilities (couldn't read, comprehend, pray, or walk) and the monotony of doing nothing. I'd had enough with the doctors, operations, procedures and the physical and mental pain. I was exhausted from constant attacks of mind that I was going to die. I wanted to get off the roller coaster. I was grateful for the rays of light but needed the sun to stay shining. I was battle-tested enough at this point and needed to come out as pure gold.

My name was changed to Jobina (Job's sister) for what seemed like forever. However, despite all that happened, I never blamed or was mad at God. In all my self-wallowing, He kept me in maintaining my pleasantness with others.

> **"When you come to the end of yourself, you find the beginning of God."**
>
> **– Author Unknown**

Have you ever felt like you were in a Job-like experience and about to break? What did you do? For me, when I couldn't do anything else, I called out The Blood of Jesus. I couldn't stop fighting even if I wanted to. And you can't either. If you are where I was, it's time to pull together and declare, "I believe and trust the Lord!" Think on those things that are pure and just. Locate the Lord by finding other spiritual outlets when you feel like you can't pray. Most importantly, seek peace and know that it's all working for the good.

> **Prayer for when you are Frustrated** – Romans 8:28 "And we know that all things work together for good to those who love God, to those who are called according to His purpose."
>
> God, thank you for the gentle reminder that all things work together for the good of them that love you! At times, it seems as if everything is chaotic, and frustration can overwhelm me. Jesus help me to remember that everything is working out for my good. You have settled it, just for me! Amen.

MIRACLES, SIGNS, AND WONDERS

> **"Miracles strengthen faith, but only God's Holy Spirit can produce faith."**
> **– John MacArthur**

Back in 2008, I went to church with my husband, and Prophet Todd Hall was the preacher for that service. He began to prophesy a few words to Bishop, but for me he said, "You will be a prophetess to the nations, but you will not be normal." Now, I heard him when he said prophetess to the nations, however I somehow missed the part about not being normal. I would hear it years later while watching the recording of his prophecy and a few others I received that were taped. I watched them for encouragement and to keep me focused on the promise.

Though in 2013 I shattered my leg, had multiple related and unrelated surgeries, was attacked in my mind by the enemy, God delivered miracles, signs, and wonders because I'm still here. There is no void of His many words.

After the accident I recall a word I received from Dr. Jacqueline Gates stating I would go near and far. I also received an additional word from Pastor Roger DeCuir stating I would be exposed to the world, and my inability to move my legs freely wouldn't be a hindrance.

Another time, I attended a conference in Atlanta, and there was a prophetic dancer there ministering. She had a banner with a man blowing a shofar and flags of different nations on the same banner. I didn't know this young lady; however, she danced near me and wrapped the banner around me saying, "You are going to the nations." Signs and wonders were around me, but I anticipated the miracle of walking freely and without pain.

The Ultimate Miracle

My husband and I attended the R.A.W. Gathering hosted by Bishop, Dr. Aretha Wilson, and Benny Hinn was the guest preacher for that night. The spirit and anointing were extremely heavy, and miracles were being performed.

I was sitting on the pulpit, and Pastor Hinn called me to him and asked what happened to my leg. I shared what happened, and he said, "You are healed," touched my face, and I was out. I'm not sure how long I was out, but when I woke, all the pain was gone, and I felt like the Tasha before the accident. The ultimate miracle is, I have some pain occasionally, but the daily and incapacitating pain I experienced is gone. JESUS DID THAT THING... YOU HEAR ME?

As I continued drawing closer, the Lord stood up stronger within me.

His Signs and Wonders

One day I was ministering at a women's ministry event. There was a young man there who I saw had a heavy spirit of depression on him that was visible to not only me but the room. The Lord led me to lay hands and pray for him in my heavenly language. With God's power, I prayed, and you could literally see the transformation taking place.

The Lord had to show me that I could still do what was necessary though Him, in my new normal. What the other signs and wonders of God's miracle working power?

1. The ability to read again. At one time my reading comprehension was off.
2. The ability to minister and preach despite my wheelchair.
3. The ability to stand without assistance.
4. The ability to drive again.
5. The ability to walk with a cane.
6. The ability to walk without a cane.
7. The ability to write this book.

Prayer for Healing – Jeremiah 17:14 "Heal me, O Lord, and I shall be healed; save me, and I shall be saved: for you are my praise."

Father, I am blessed by the healing power of your glory resting on my life! I thank you for every broken place that I thought would never be healed. For your word is true, you said: "that you would bring health to my body and nourishment to my bones" (Proverbs 3:8), and for that, I thank YOU! Amen.

MY CONCLUSIONS

CLOSURE

What is my definition of brokenness? Being forcibly pushed into the unknown. I believe I was pushed there at a young age due to the absence of my father through the years. Who would've thought the literal shattering of my limb would stir up and bring forward the broken place dormant in my life for many years? That place was the lack of a relationship with my father.

My parents divorced when I was eight years old. After their separation, I had a sporadic relationship with my dad. Growing up, I would talk to or see him every other year, if that. I am his only child who many times felt rejected due to his choices concerning me. He would have two other families, due to marriages, after his marriage to my mother. I felt like he put everyone (their children) in front of me. I didn't receive birthday cards, holiday gifts, or anything else you can think a father would do for his daughter.

My belief is he stayed away from me because I reminded him of my mother, and he had an issue with women in general based on his behavior and mindset. I never rejected him but resolved our situation to 'it is what it is' type of relationship. The Lord kept me, and I am grateful his rejection didn't send me down a destructive path many girls take when that happens.

The Mending

When the accident occurred, my husband called my father and told him what happened. He came to see me in the hospital for a few days, and it jumpstarted the mending of our relationship. Although a man of few words, chauvinistic, stern, and believed those younger didn't know anything, I did my best to love and honor all he was and wasn't. Interestingly, in all his views and beliefs, there was one person who had a hold on him and did all she could to keep us from forming a relationship. I will get to that in a moment, but he did begin to call more and check on me.

In 2014, my father came to my home in New York to visit. This would be the first time we spent the night in the same house in over thirty years. I could tell he was nervous, and he brought his cousin along to keep him company. It was my birthday, and yearly my family came to my house to celebrate.

On the day of my birthday, he cooked on the grill and wouldn't let anyone touch it. During gifts time, he presented me with a Michael Kors bag. I hadn't received anything from him since I was eight. For a moment, I felt like daddy's little girl, and it was beautiful to see his thoughtfulness.

In the spirit and his countenance, I could see he was ill. That day, he apologized to my mother and me as well for his actions, mistakes and his part in us not being a family anymore. His visit yielded calls at least twice per week, but our calls were short.

The 'Step Monster'

In one of our conversations, my father finally shared he was sick. I made it a point not to pry and received information on his health as it was provided. I visited him where he lived when I could, but the drama with The 'Step Monster' was a lot to deal with. Calling her a monster is not to disrespect her but to speak to the spirit she carries. Keep reading.

My dad convinced my husband and me to stay at his home. His wife had what I call fake hospitality. Honey, my discernment was on 150% being around her. Not sure why, but she didn't like me. However, when we visited, she gave an E.G.O.T. performance (look it up) in front of my father. We felt uncomfortable and decided not to spend the night in their home whenever we visited.

My father received the news that the doctors no longer could do anything for him. When I visited, I wanted to do whatever made my father happy as his health continued to deteriorate. When I visited him, I would rub his feet and sing. He asked me to purchase him some sweatsuits to lounge in, and I granted his request. The Step Monster had a problem with it and made a comment saying, "Instead of buying clothes, you need to give him money." She told people I was a horrible daughter, a so-called big-time preacher who only wanted money from my father. The rumors she spread were crazy, but I ignored her and those who fueled her foolishness.

She had two sons, one who appeared to have a problem with me just like his mother. The other son was nice, respectful and didn't act in the manner of his mother. We developed a friendly rapport with one another.

One day the 'not nice son' called me asking if my grandmother and aunt (dad's sister) would give $3,000 each to go toward the care of my father. My dad was a veteran who was eligible for benefits and hospice care, but his wife decided she wanted to be his caretaker and ask us to pay for it. Of course, we said no only to find later they were trying to get money for my dad's funeral. Why? Not sure because he had insurance, his own money, and they already had the location to be buried near one another.

You may ask about the significance of my sharing this. Trust me it will all make sense once I finish the story.

The End Is Near

I received a call stating my dad was in an any day now stage of passing. I had the opportunity to talk to him the day before his actual passing. I told him I loved him. It was sad because we only had a few years together at that point. However, I had peace of knowing I did all that I could to restore the relationship between us.

My dad's passing was not only the closure to the relationship but an ending of being in brokenness for many years. I learned a few things about myself while he was alive and especially when he passed. The biggest lessons were.

- ✓ Thick skin is required to get through life. Without going into too much detail, I went through a lot with my father as a young child and overcame it all. Stay tuned for the tell-all book about our story.
- ✓ If I could overcome rejection from my father, I could overcome anything.
- ✓ I gained a higher level of patience and tolerance in our short time together.
- ✓ His passing meant the person who broke me as a little girl could never hurt me again.

A Closed Chapter

When notified my dad passed away, I waited a day to contact his wife and give her some time to breathe. When I called, she answered the phone and had a nicety tone in her voice. I called the next day to check on her and see if any arrangements were made; she didn't answer.

Later that day, I received a call from the 'not nice son' son asking questions on my involvement in the funeral. My spirit said his inquiry was rooted in asking for money. I said I would follow her lead. I wanted to be respectful and psyched myself into thinking she would do the same since I was her husband's only child.

I reached out to ask if I could do a tribute at the funeral, but she didn't answer. I text the question, and she responded saying she didn't want me or my husband to do anything on the program. There you go, hurt, and rejected again. However, this would be the last time. For clarity, a human monster is someone cruel and is keenly aware of the harm they're causing. They have no clear reason for their actions, but the actions are rooted in selfish desires.

The day of the wake, The Step Monster acknowledged us by telling us to introduce ourselves to everyone; we ignored the gesture. The nice son insisted that I have a chance to speak during that time. She agreed but said that's it. I couldn't sing. My husband had a few words as well.

The day of the funeral, as my family sat on one side and her family on the other, we were asked to move our seats in the front row. Keep in mind who was sitting in the seats; his mother (my grandmother), and his sisters (my aunts), my husband, me, and other members of my father's family. A few people intervened, and we remained in our seats. She had her entire family on the program to sing, do scripture, and her mean son officiated the service. When reading the cards and condolences, proclamations sent from New York on my behalf were read as well, which made her livid.

It was time to go to the burial, and my father opted to be placed in a mausoleum. As we left to join the processional, I was already parked behind the hearse but purposely made to wait until many cars pulled out first. When we arrived at the location, my grandmother (his mother) and I managed to get a seat while the committal was done. Once they closed the tomb, I got up, walked to my car, got in, and never looked back.

The chapter of brokenness was closed! The days of disrespect were over! I received a letter from his estate and didn't answer. I didn't want or need anything from that situation. The Lord did His perfect work for the time we had together. My dad was gone, and I was done in Jesus' name!

Prayer for when you have closed a chapter – James 1:2-4
"My brethren, count it all joy when you fall into various trials, knowing that the testing of your faith produces patience. But let patience have its perfect work, that you may be perfect and complete lacking nothing."

Father, I thank you for every door that has been closed due to challenges, brokenness, and heartbreak. Lord, I know you watched everything that has taken place in my life, and I am grateful that every experience has had its perfect work displayed. So Jesus, I count it all joy, for it works for me! Amen.

IT'S MY TIME

As I write this closing portion, I realize that the Lord delivered me from physical, mental, and emotional anguish. I am an Overcomer! Creating this book was challenging because I was apprehensive about revealing myself and the struggles I encountered; I'm a private person.

Brokenness brought out parts of me I didn't know existed. I have a new revelation on the word longsuffering. The trial awakened my strength to endure and brought me closer to God in a new way. In that time of sitting still, I had no choice but to see all the places that were broken in my life.

I'm now 'Broken' with a different mindset of one who is open to the pouring of God. I'm no longer in that dark space and have no intention of going back. It's my time to rise, shine, live, and fly as God intended. Tasha is a new person mentally, spiritually and physically. Although I walk with a slight limp, I continue to embrace who I am in this new journey.

Mentally, my mind, that couldn't comprehend is renewed. I make decisions carefully. I am more reflective about where I've been and where I'm going. Spiritually, I let God take care of what I normally would. I've stopped making assumptions about people, places and things. I'm able to pray and flow freely in the prophetic gift He has given me. I embrace the joy of the Lord and look for opportunities to laugh despite how I am feeling on a particular day. Physically, I'm a risk-taker. Meaning, I am open to taking more chances and exercising my faith in God when it comes to ideas and witty inventions. I am wide open to the infinite possibilities of God like never before.

Praise God, I finished school and receive my Master of Science in Organizational Leadership.

During this writing process, I conversed with a young lady who previously received a diagnosis of Breast Cancer. Although walking firmly in her healing for several years, she is often asked if she is worried the cancer will come back. Her answer is always the same, "I can't live my life worried about that. God has delivered, so I am out of that season!"

Why am I sharing her testimony? Too many confessors of Jesus Christ opt to stay in the place where God brought them out. There is a stench of fear to celebrate or humbly brag about the goodness and keeping power of God. It's time to rise from people, out of the ashes, and move toward the words spoken over your life.

If the Lord has done or is doing something miraculous in your life, walk in it with power, authority, with the anointing, and without fear. The moment of 'your time' doesn't have to end at the moment but can gain momentum to the next level in God. I encourage you to live life to the fullest of His glory. Why? Because it's our time!

Prayer for IT'S MY TIME – Psalm 102:13 "You will arise and have mercy on Zion; For the time to favor her, yes the set time, has come."

God, I thank you for this is My Set Time! Thank you for pulling me up out of my brokenness and reviving me with time and life! Thank you for restoring my health, my mind, my emotions, and my spirit to align with your will and purpose. Thank you for the fresh oil and fresh wind upon my life! God, Thank You, Thank You, Thank You for you have declared that I shall arise, I shall have mercy, and I shall have Favor, for My Time has Come! IT'S MY TIME! Amen.

PROPHETESS
TASHA S. BASTON

Breaking Boundaries, Building Up Believers, Prophetess Tasha Sharron Baston fashioned in divine wisdom, grace, and obedience to God's will has been chosen by God to preach the infallible word and truths of Jesus Christ. A servant leader and revelatory expounder of God's word, Prophetess Baston serves as the Leading Lady and Assistant Pastor, alongside her husband and pastor Bishop Dr. Michael A. Baston at St. Luke Cathedral in Laurelton, New York. Together, they established Called to the Nations Covenant Churches International, Inc. (CNCCI). CNCCI is a multi-denominational Kingdom focused community of covenant churches, pastors, and ministries who hold spiritual authority and flow with the purpose of empowering leaders and ministries of influence. The goal is to assist them in effectively impacting their congregations, communities, regions, and world for the Kingdom of God.

Prophetess Baston is the Founder and Host of the Breaker Anointing Experience (BAE), a powerful conference, presenting a plethora of seminars and services aimed at helping men, women, and children overcome barriers to lead successful lives through Jesus Christ. Prophetess Baston is the CEO and Founder of Women Impacting the Next Generation of Sisters (W.I.N.G.S) which provides mentorship, counseling, personal and professional seminars, and services toward the empowerment of women throughout the New York Tri-State area. After nearly ten years of faithful kingdom assignment and ministry as both Evangelist and Elder, at the leading of the Holy Spirit and wise counsel and release of her husband and Pastor, Prophetess Baston humbly accepted her call to prophetic ministry. And on May 5, 2012, she was affirmed, consecrated and commissioned to operate in the governmental office of Prophet by her apostolic father in ministry, and the Emeritus Pastor of the New Greater Bethel Ministries, Inc., the late Apostle Dr. John H. Boyd, Sr.

Prophetess Baston is the Founder of Tasha Baston Ministries—an itinerant ministry where she travels extensively preaching, teaching, mentoring, and counseling God's people equipping and empowering them through the joy, peace, and love of Jesus Christ. And in 2017, she released her highly anticipated single entitled "I Give You All the Praise."

Prophetess Baston holds a Master of Science (M.S.) in Organizational Leadership from Nyack College Rockland, New York, and a Bachelor of Business Administration (B.B.A.) in Management from Berkley College Manhattan, New York. Additionally, she has been awarded an Honorary Doctor of Divinity (D.D.) from Anointed by God Ministries Alliance and Seminary Brooklyn, NY. Prophetess Baston resides in Long Island, New York with her loving husband, Bishop Dr. Michael A. Baston.

@tashabastonministries

@tashabastonministries_